THE POETRY OF TANTALUM

The Poetry of Tantalum

Walter the Educator

Silent King Books

SILENT KING BOOKS

SKB

Copyright © 2024 by Walter the Educator

All rights reserved. No part of this book may be reproduced in any manner whatsoever without written permission except in the case of brief quotations embodied in critical articles and reviews.

First Printing, 2024

Disclaimer
This book is a literary work; poems are not about specific persons, locations, situations, and/or circumstances unless mentioned in a historical context. This book is for entertainment and informational purposes only. The author and publisher offer this information without warranties expressed or implied. No matter the grounds, neither the author nor the publisher will be accountable for any losses, injuries, or other damages caused by the reader's use of this book. The use of this book acknowledges an understanding and acceptance of this disclaimer.

dedicated to all the chemistry lovers,
like myself, across the world

TANTALUM

In the periodic table's vast domain,

TANTALUM

Amidst the elements that reign,

TANTALUM

Tantalum stands, a gleaming prize,

TANTALUM

With properties that mesmerize.
TANTALUM

From the heart of the Earth it's drawn,

TANTALUM

In mines where shadows faintly spawn,

TANTALUM

Tantalum, noble and rare,

TANTALUM

In nature's depths, it's found with care.

TANTALUM

Atomic number seventy-three,

TANTALUM

A lustrous metal, strong and free,

TANTALUM

Its name derived from Greek myth's lore,

TANTALUM

Tantalus, punished evermore.

TANTALUM

Within its core, electrons dance,

TANTALUM

In orbits, they gracefully prance,

TANTALUM

A valence shell with trusty eight,

TANTALUM

Tantalum's bonds, they never abate.

TANTALUM

Resistant to corrosion's bite,

TANTALUM

In acids' grasp, it stands upright,

TANTALUM

Its surface gleams with steadfast grace,

TANTALUM

Defying time, in any space.

TANTALUM

In capacitors, it finds its place,

TANTALUM

Storing charge with steadfast grace,

TANTALUM

Electronics hum with its might,

TANTALUM

Tantalum's presence, a guiding light.

TANTALUM

From spacecraft soaring to the stars,

TANTALUM

To gadgets small as matchbox cars,

TANTALUM

Tantalum's touch, a silent hand,

TANTALUM

Enriching lives across the land.

TANTALUM

In medical devices, it plays its part,

TANTALUM

Mending bodies, healing heart,

TANTALUM

Implants of hope, made strong and true,

TANTALUM

Tantalum, we owe much to you.

TANTALUM

But let us not forget the cost,

TANTALUM

The toll on lands where it is lost,

TANTALUM

In regions torn by strife and greed,

TANTALUM

Tantalum's story, one of need.

TANTALUM

So here's to Tantalum, noble and rare,

TANTALUM

With strength and beauty, beyond compare,

TANTALUM

May its story teach us to tread,

TANTALUM

With reverence, where resources are spread.

TANTALUM

ABOUT THE CREATOR

Walter the Educator is one of the pseudonyms for Walter Anderson. Formally educated in Chemistry, Business, and Education, he is an educator, an author, a diverse entrepreneur, and he is the son of a disabled war veteran. "Walter the Educator" shares his time between educating and creating. He holds interests and owns several creative projects that entertain, enlighten, enhance, and educate, hoping to inspire and motivate you.

Follow, find new works, and stay up to date with Walter the Educator™ at WaltertheEducator.com

www.ingramcontent.com/pod-product-compliance
Lightning Source LLC
La Vergne TN
LVHW010412070526
838199LV00064B/5276